S is for S'mores

A Camping Alphabet

Written by Helen Foster James and Illustrated by Lita Judge

Special thanks to all the terrific kids who modeled for these illustrations.

—Lita Judge

Sleeping Bear Press™
310 North Main Street, Suite 300
Chelsea, MI 48118
www.sleepingbearpress.com

© 2007 Thomson Gale, a part of the Thomson Corporation.

Thomson, Star Logo and Sleeping Bear Press are trademarks
and Gale is a registered trademark used herein under license.

Printed and bound in China.

First Edition

10 9 8 7 6 5 4 3 2 1

Library of Congress Cataloging-in-Publication Data

James, Helen Foster, 1951-
S is for s'mores : a camping alphabet / written by Helen Foster James;
illustrated by Lita Judge.
p. cm.
Summary: "Introduces camping from A to Z using poetry, prose, and illustrations
in a children's picture book. Includes information on beach camping, canyons,
foliage, camping gear, John Muir, Juliette Gordon Low, and more"
—Provided by publisher.
ISBN-13: 978-1-58536-302-5
ISBN-10: 1-58536-302-2
1. Camping—Juvenile literature. 2. Alphabet books. I. Judge, Lita, ill. II. Title.
GV192.2.J36 2007
796.54—dc22   2006027138

A backpack full of thanks to
Sleeping Bear Press and my husband Bob.

For My Camping Buddies—
Happy Trails to You.

HELEN

🚶‍♂️🚶‍♀️

To the wildlife who share their homes
with us when we camp.

LITA

Aa

A is for Adventure.
Let's camp from A to Z.
On mountains and deserts or beaches,
if you want to have fun, follow me!

Campers enjoy the outdoors from a desert floor to a mountain peak or by a lake. They hike, fish, climb rocks, watch wild animals, examine wildflowers, listen for birds, canoe, kayak, and more. "Home" for the night might be a tent, trailer, or motor home.

Camping became more popular when cars became affordable. Campers packed their cars full of gear and headed for adventure. They drove to places they couldn't visit when they used trains or steamships for transportation.

Roads were primitive in the early 1900s, but campers liked "roughing it." Soon everyone liked camping. Automaker Henry Ford, inventor Thomas Edison, tire manufacturer Harvey Firestone, and President Warren Harding went on a camping trip together in the Blue Ridge Mountains in 1921.

Before camping, it's important to learn how to respect nature, keep safe, and have fun with family and friends. Read on to learn how to be a "happy camper."

B is for our Beach camp
with the water's edge nearby.
We paddle, swim, and fish
beneath a bright blue sky.

Beach camps can be near an ocean, river, or lake. The gear that campers take depends on their water activities. Campers who fish, for example, take fishing poles, line, and bait. Every boater must keep safe by taking and wearing a life jacket or PFD (Personal Flotation Device).

Canoeists paddle their canoe to see scenery and get exercise. Some paddle from one campsite to another each day or even from one lake to another with their gear tucked safely in their canoe.

Minnesota's Voyageurs National Park was named for French-Canadian trappers who traveled long ago in birch bark canoes. Today its lakes and bays are favorite canoeing and kayaking areas.

At California's Channel Islands National Park campers arrive in boats. Permits and reservations are needed to camp at these primitive campsites. Snorkelers pack swimsuit, fins, mask, and snorkel in gear bags for camping on nearby privately owned Catalina Island.

Lake Mead is one of the world's largest artificially created lakes and a favorite boating, fishing, and swimming area. It's located on the Arizona-Nevada border.

Bb

C c

C is for the Canyons
and few are as great as the "Grand."
Slowly carved by nature's knives
of water, wind, and sand.

Arizona's Grand Canyon National Park is one of the world's most amazing canyons. The Colorado River helped carve this giant chasm. It's nearly a mile deep in some places. There are many hiking trails in the park. Some visitors ride a mule to the bottom to camp. Others raft through the canyon on the Colorado River and camp by the river's edge. The Grand Canyon is a World Heritage Site.

Utah's Bryce Canyon National Park and Zion National Park are two other well-known canyon areas. They are famous for their beauty and amazing geological formations. There are many canyons with trails and sights to explore in campgrounds in almost every state and around the world.

Boots are an important piece of gear for hiking up and down canyons. Sneakers are fine for some camping trips, but for more strenuous hikes it is important to wear boots that give ankle support and have soles that grip rocks. Hikers need to save energy to hike back up a canyon after they've hiked down.

D is for the Desert.
Look carefully and see
the many plants and animals
that live here wild and free.

The desert is a fascinating camping environment. Campers must look carefully to notice the variety of flowers and animals that live in the desert. Different animals and plants live in specific desert areas and have adaptations. Some desert animals, for example, are nocturnal and are awake in the evening to hunt for food when it's cooler.

Deserts can be extremely hot in the summer, making them favorite camping areas in winter and spring. In spring, desert floors burst with a carpet of colorful wildflowers and blooming cacti when there is a perfect combination of rain and timing. Flowers may be as small as a pinhead or large like the ocotillo's (ah-ko-TEE-oh) bright red flowers.

Arroyos are sandy river washes that may look like a comfortable tent spot, but they can flood quickly during a thunderstorm. So always avoid camping in low areas where water can collect.

Some desert campsites have drinkable water, but if not, be sure to take at least one gallon of water per person per day, and drink it to avoid becoming dehydrated. Juice and soda may seem thirst quenching, but water is essential.

Desert campers need light colored clothing to keep cool during the day and layers of clothing to put on for nippy nights. Desert campers always pack sunscreen, sunglasses, and a wide brim hat for sun protection.

Death Valley National Park is the driest, hottest, and lowest location in North America.

Joshua Tree National Park is where the unusual looking Joshua trees grow. They grow slowly but can live more than 200 years. They look like they have oddly shaped, outstretched arms.

Many desert areas are protected to preserve their fragile environment, but other areas are set aside for recreational fun with dune buggies and other off-road vehicles.

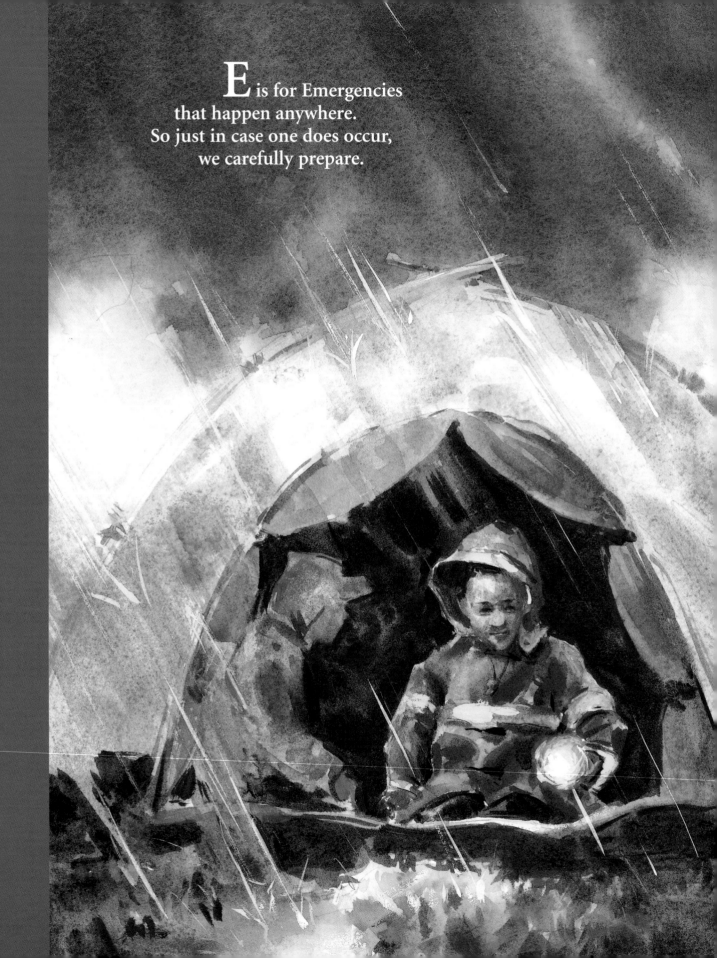

E e

E is for Emergencies
that happen anywhere.
So just in case one does occur,
we carefully prepare.

Here are ten "essentials" campers must pack to keep safe and be prepared in an emergency.

- sun protection (sunscreen, sunglasses, hat with a brim, lip protection)
- flashlight or headlight (and extra, fresh batteries)
- whistle
- map
- compass (and know how to use it)
- extra food and water
- waterproof matches (in a waterproof container) and fire starter (such as a candle)
- first aid kit
- pocket knife or multiuse tool
- extra clothing (and rain gear)

A first aid kit with bandages, moleskin, and antiseptic ointment helps with minor problems including blisters, scrapes, and insect bites. Many campers add insect repellent to their list of essentials. For safety, keep a whistle handy on a cord around your neck. A whistle signals that help is needed, so blow it only in an emergency and then stay put. A lantern lights a campsite for everyone, but each person needs a personal flashlight. Headlights are handy. Some campers consider toilet paper the 11th essential.

Campers enjoy the beauty of changing leaves in each season. Deciduous trees, like maple, oak, birch, and aspen, lose their leaves in the fall, after first turning brilliant colors of scarlet, orange, or gold. "Leaf peepers" search for the locations of the most beautiful fall leaves.

Vermont is known for its maple trees and their glorious fall colors. The Kancamagus Highway in New Hampshire's White Mountain National Forest winds through vibrant views of autumn leaves.

Conifers, such as pine, spruce, and hemlock trees, are cone-bearing trees and keep their leaves or needles all year. Forests are a mix of deciduous and conifer trees.

Leaves have different shapes—like a feather, mitten, or fan. Become a leaf expert and look closely at leaves and notice their shapes. Although most leaves are lovely and safe to touch, learn how to recognize and avoid poison oak, poison ivy, and other irritating plants. Pants help protect skin from poisonous plants. A helpful poison oak/poison ivy rule is "Leaves of three—let it be." If you see it, don't touch it.

F is for the Foliage
with changing looks in every season
(spring and summer, fall and winter).
Would you like to know the reason?

Gg

Camping gear includes shelter, cooking supplies and food, clothing, personal needs, and essentials (see **E** for a list). The gear campers need depends on their camping activities, the camp's location, the season, and weather. It's smart to make a gear list before packing to make sure you take everything you'll need. Always pack just enough gear to keep safe and comfortable.

Many campers use a tent for their shelter. You *pitch* a tent to put it up and *strike* it to take it down. The top layer of a tent is a rain fly and it protects campers from rain and snow. Poles hold a tent up and pegs (or stakes) keep a tent in place even in gusty winds. A ground cloth under a tent helps keep it clean and dry.

Tents can be small in size and just big enough for one person to a spacious tent for an entire family. There are different shapes like a dome, A-frame, or a "pup tent." The type of tent you use depends on the type of camping you will be doing and the time of year you will be doing it. Temporary shelters called bivouacs (biv-waks) are made by placing a tarp over a low tree branch or over a rope tied between two trees.

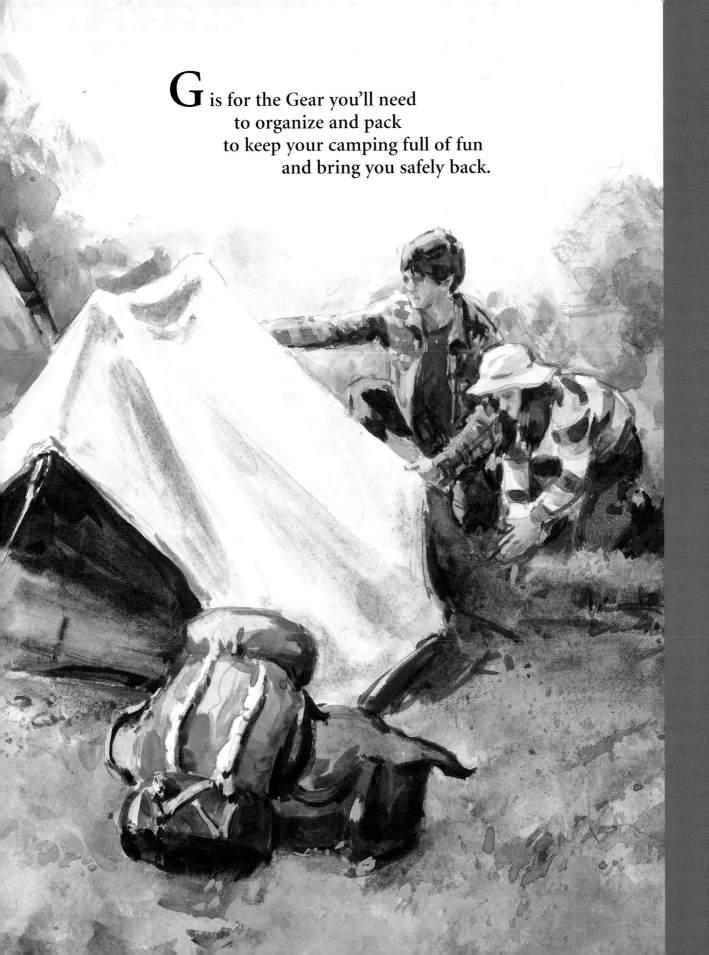

G is for the Gear you'll need
to organize and pack
to keep your camping full of fun
and bring you safely back.

Camping clothes should be made of fabrics that protect from the sun, wind, and rain. Take clothes to wear over each other in layers. This makes it easy to add clothing as the day becomes colder or to remove when it gets warmer. Brightly colored clothes make it easy to spot a hiker on a trail. Sturdy boots and clean, dry socks keep a hiker's feet comfortable. Always pack rain gear to be prepared for sudden thunderstorms and weather changes.

Personal gear, like a toothbrush and comb, can be stowed in a "ditty bag" or "stuff sack." Sleeping bags and down jackets can be stuffed and stored in a stuff sack to make them compact and keep them clean. A stuff sack stuffed with a soft jacket makes a comfy pillow.

Some campers take a cell phone, but remember they don't always work in camping areas.

H is for the Hikers
whose boots protect their feet
while hiking on a rocky trail
or through the desert's heat.

Some campers "hit the trail" on hikes near their campsite. A daypack holds their essentials. A hiking stick helps keep a hiker balanced, especially when tired or crossing a stream. Always hike with an adult buddy and make sure someone at camp knows where you're going and when you'll return.

Backpackers take longer trips with gear they need for the entire trip in their backpack. Their pack is large enough to hold all their gear, but as light as possible to be comfortable. They even pack a tiny stove and lightweight, freeze-dried (dehydrated) food.

Hiking trails are very different. At Hawai'i Volcanoes National Park hikers cross lava formed by an ancient volcano. In Olympic National Park hikers walk through a temperate rain forest that gets 12 to 14 feet of rain each year.

The Pacific Crest Trail, a National Scenic Trail, travels from Mexico to Canada. It makes its way 2,650 miles through California, Oregon, and Washington, passing through six of the seven North American eco-zones. Hikers who complete an entire National Scenic Trail are called "thru-hikers."

Insects are amazing and there are plenty to see on a camping trip. Insects have six legs (three pairs) and a body that is divided into three main parts: head, thorax, and abdomen. Most insects have wings and a pair of antennae. Some people think ticks, spiders, and scorpions are insects, but they're not.

Butterflies have brightly colored wings and intricate patterns. Did you know they have taste sensors on their feet? Hear that mosquito's hum? That's its wings beating 500 to 1,000 times a second. If you were as strong as an ant you could pick up a car. Be sure to store camping food away from those hungry ants!

Campers may encounter pesky insects such as ants, chiggers, or mosquitoes, but only one percent of all insects is harmful. If you react to insect bites, remember to take your allergy treatment. Some mosquitoes can be avoided by staying away from stagnant pools of water. Insect repellent, long sleeves, and sometimes even wearing a net over your head will help keep bugs from bugging you.

I is for the Insects
like butterflies and bees,
or ladybugs and dragonflies,
and itty-bitty fleas.

Naturalist John Muir (1838-1914) loved exploring the wilderness. He's called the "Father of our National Parks" for his conservation work to protect wildlife areas.

Muir was born in Scotland and his family immigrated to America in 1849. Muir hiked thousands of miles through forests, mountains, and deserts and wrote about his adventures. He encouraged others to respect the outdoors and promoted wilderness preservation. He helped form the Sierra Club and became its first president.

Muir slept under the stars in Yosemite Valley. In 2005 California's new state quarter featured John Muir with his beloved Yosemite National Park.

This World Heritage Site's gigantic trees, plunging waterfalls, and deep valley make it a spectacular camping area. Visitors hike, rock climb, scramble to the top of Half Dome, and explore the nearby backcountry.

"Climb the mountains and get their good tidings." —John Muir

J is for John and for Juliette.
They both loved nature and planned
for people who camp in the great outdoors
to protect and cherish this land.

Juliette Gordon Low (1860-1927) was the founder of the Girl Scouts. She was born in Savannah, Georgia, and was called "Daisy." She married an Englishman and moved to England where she met Sir Robert Baden-Powell in 1911. He was the founder of the Boy Scouts and Girl Guides, and she admired his work. A year later she returned to the United States.

Juliette wanted to do something special with her life. One day she made an important phone call to a friend and announced, "I've got something for the girls of Savannah, and all of America, and all the world, and we're going to start it tonight!" On March 12, 1912, she gathered 18 girls to create the first troop of American Girl Guides. Her niece was the first registered member. The group's name was changed to Girl Scouts the following year.

Juliette Low's home in Savannah is now a National Center of Girl Scouts of the USA.

K is for our Kitchen.
It doesn't have a door.
No roof or walls surround it
and solid ground its floor.

Campers prepare food in a "kitchen," but it doesn't look like a kitchen at home. A campfire or camp stove replaces a microwave, stove, and oven. An ice chest substitutes for a refrigerator. The sink might be a dishpan. A mess kit is an efficient group of nesting dishes. Camp cuisine might be roasting hot dogs over a campfire or cooking with a Dutch oven (heavy pot with a close-fitting lid).

In bear country, campers protect their food and scented items by placing them in bear storage containers or hanging them in stuff sacks in trees out of the reach of hungry bears. Never store food in a tent or car. Help protect bears by keeping them wild and not dependent on human food.

Many campsites have potable (drinkable) water, but sometimes campers must bring their own water. It's usually not safe to drink water from rivers or springs until it has been purified. Water may look clean and clear, but it can contain microscopic organisms or minerals that cause sickness. Campers should always ask park officials if the water is safe to drink.

L is for the Lupine
in patches near the trail
with vibrant colored petals
and a sweet and fragrant smell.

Lupine is just one wildflower that puts on a beautiful spring show. It grows all across the United States. Almost every camping area has a variety of wildflowers. Each spring wildflowers cover the land with a rainbow of color depending on the area, elevation, precipitation, and other conditions. Take time to find them, learn their names, and notice their unique characteristics. Be careful to avoid stepping on fragile flowers when hiking.

Thousands of wildflowers are found in the United States alone. Plants are important to us and are a natural resource. Never pick wildflowers. Many are endangered. They are part of the area's ecosystem. Always leave them alone so they can grow, go to seed, and blossom again next season.

Rocky Mountain National Park in Colorado has 60 peaks over 12,000 feet high. It is home to many animals, and in June and July visitors enjoy a spectacular show of wildflowers.

The Spring Wildflower Pilgrimage is an annual event of the Great Smoky Mountains National Park. This park is located in North Carolina and Tennessee and is a World Heritage Site.

Ll

Mountains and their forests are favorite camping destinations. Higher elevations usually mean cooler weather. Campers should pack warm clothing and always remember to take rain gear. Sometimes campers prepare for dramatic changes in altitude by slowing down their activities when they first arrive at a high elevation. Some people get drowsy or even ill at high altitudes. Always tell an adult if you do not feel well.

An instrument called an altimeter gives the elevation in feet (or meters) above sea level. When hikers start their hike, they check their elevation (or altitude) with an altimeter. When they reach the highest (or lowest) point of their hike, they check the altimeter again. By comparing the two elevations they find the elevation gain or loss made on their hike.

The Appalachian Mountains are the oldest mountain chain in North America. North America's highest mountain, Mount McKinley (also called Denali) is 20,320 feet tall and is located in Alaska's Denali National Park and Preserve. Wyoming's Grand Teton National Park was formed by earthquakes over the past 13 million years. More than 100 alpine lakes are in the backcountry and the Teton Range is 40 miles long.

M m

M is for the Mountains
where bear cubs play and eagles soar,
where campers hike so close to clouds
and ask for nothing more.

N n

N is for the Night Sky
far from the city's lights.
Find Polaris pointing north
and other famous sights.

Many people know about noise and water pollution, but there's also light pollution—excess light caused by humans. City lights make it difficult to see stars, but campers can see a dazzling display of stars on clear, cloudless nights.

Long ago, people gave names to groups of stars (constellations) that formed shapes. A star chart labels these constellations. The Big and Little Dipper are two that are easy to find. The Little Dipper is important because Polaris, the North Star, is at the end of its handle. On a clear night, campers can use stars to orient themselves and find "north." Stars, shooting stars, comets, and planets are easier to view with a telescope or binoculars.

The moon has a 29.5-day cycle. When it is waxing, or getting bigger, the crescent faces left and when waning the crescent faces right. The moon grows from no moon, to full moon, to no moon again during each cycle. Some hikers like night hikes—especially when the moon is full. Campers bundle up and take a flashlight to hike at night.

Boy Scouts, Girl Scouts, Camp Fire, YMCA, YWCA, the Sierra Club, and other similar organizations teach beginners new skills and help advanced campers improve their skills. As campers gain skills they plan longer, strenuous camping trips. These organizations protect our environment by teaching about nature and how each person makes a difference. The Sierra Club is the oldest environmental organization in America. Chapters in the United States and Canada organize classes, outings, and trips throughout the world.

Some schools organize camping trips for students during the school year. The "great outdoors" becomes the students' classroom. They become familiar with the flora and fauna (flowers and animals) that live in nearby wilderness areas. They learn about diurnal and nocturnal animals (animals that are awake during the day or evening). Students learn basic camping skills. They work with their classmates to appreciate and protect the environment and act responsibly with the earth's resources.

National Wildlife Week is sponsored each year by the National Wildlife Federation. It was started to help people enjoy the outdoors and to encourage conservation efforts.

O
o

O is for the Organizations
that share and teach their skills
to those of us who love to camp
and hike among the hills.

P is for the many Parks.
Let's pick a destination,
then pack our gear, and go explore
for a wonderful vacation.

There are great campsites in national, state, regional, and private parks. Upon arrival, stop at the park's visitor center for up-to-date safety information and an overview of the park. Schedules of campfire programs and nature hikes are posted there and on campsite bulletin boards. This information helps visitors decide what to do during their stay. Campsites can be reserved in advance online or by contacting a park. Some campsites are "first-come, first-served." It's smart to plan ahead when camping at popular campgrounds.

Acadia National Park was the first national park established east of the Mississippi River. Located on the rugged coastline of Maine, it has mountains, woodlands, lakes, and ponds to explore.

Banff National Park was Canada's first and the world's third national park. Meltwater from Victoria Glacier mixes with glacial silt and rock dust to give Banff's Lake Louise its beautiful blue-green color. The Canadian Rocky Mountain Parks (including Banff, Jasper, Yoho, and Kootenay) are a World Heritage Site.

The United States has over 50 national parks. More than 120 countries have established over 1,500 national parks throughout the world.

Q is for Quiet.
Take time to listen—what's that you hear?
A caw, a chirp, a little coo?
Is it far away or near?

Listen carefully. Do you hear those birds? They make interesting calls and songs. Campers might hear the squawk of a blue jay, the mournful call of a mourning dove, or the busy pecking of a woodpecker. Birds make noises with their wings and bills. **Q** is also for Quail—a bird you might see running and scratching the ground for food. What is your state's bird? Have you ever seen or heard one?

Binoculars and a field guide are important bird-watching gear. Field guides identify birds with photographs and descriptions. Binoculars help "birders" examine a bird's coloring, beak, and claws. An ornithologist is a zoologist who studies birds, but bird-watching (or "birding") is also a hobby. Some birders keep a list of their bird sightings.

Birds aren't the only animals making noise. There might be toads singing and croaking from their watery home. At night, the yip and howl of coyotes may break the evening quiet. Be still and listen to the sounds of animals. Remember you are a visitor to nature.

Rangers perform many different duties that are important for campers. They preserve and protect national parks. They help keep visitors safe. They teach visitors about protected areas' natural and cultural resources. Their job requires that they love the environment and work well with people.

When national parks began, only men were rangers but sometimes their wives helped them with their duties. The first women rangers were called "Rangerettes." Clare Marie Hodges (Wolfson) and Helene Wilson were the first women hired. They were hired in 1918 as temporary employees. Now both men and women are rangers.

Rangers need our cooperation. Everyone can help by learning about national parks, forests, and other protected lands. All of us can help protect the beauty, history, and culture of an area for future visitors. You might want to become a Junior Ranger and learn about a park's wildlife, history, and geology, and how to protect a park. Some parks offer online Junior Ranger programs. National parks have activities to complete to receive a badge, patch, or Junior Ranger certificate.

R r

R is for the Rangers
who teach us all to care
for the beauty and the wildlife
of all the land we share.

A campfire is a favorite evening camping activity. Friends and family gather at the end of a busy day to tell their favorite stories, jokes, and to sing songs. Everyone likes to learn a new song, story, or joke to share around the campfire.

Campfires should be made only by adults and only where campfires are allowed. Campsites usually have fire rings so do not make a new one. Children should never use matches or fire starters. Never make a fire where fires are not recommended or if the fire danger is high. Campfires should be placed a safe distance from tents and overhanging tree branches. Be careful around campfires. Be sure a fire is completely out (or dead) before leaving it. Carelessness can start a destructive fire.

Campfire builders will need wood. They'll also need kindling—small sticks, wood shavings, dry leaves, grass, or needles. Not all parks allow the gathering of fire materials so first check and follow all park rules. Some campgrounds provide or sell wood. Once the fire is started, small wood is gradually added to keep the fire burning. Do not use green or freshly cut wood. As a fire grows, larger pieces of wood are added. Adults may want to bring a hatchet to cut firewood. Keep a bucket of water and a shovel nearby to control the fire.

S s

S is for Stories and Songs
    to share when the day is done.
We enjoy our campfire's warmth
    and make yummy s'mores for some fun.

S is also for s'mores. What are s'mores? They are a yummy dessert sandwich made at a campfire. Why are they called s'mores? Because when campers eat one, they always say I want "some more." No one knows who first thought of this delicious treat, but the first known recorded recipe was in the 1927 book *Tramping and Trailing with the Girl Scouts*.

August 10 is National S'mores Day, but every camping trip is a fun time to enjoy this tasty treat. S'mores are easy to make with an adult's help.

S'mores Recipe

Ingredients:
- Graham crackers
- Chocolate candy bar (thin type)
- Marshmallows (big type)

Equipment:
- A roasting stick or long fork
- A campfire
- An adult to help you

1. Get two graham crackers.
2. Put a thin chocolate candy bar on one of the graham crackers.
3. Put a marshmallow on a roasting stick and roast until it's a toasty, golden brown.
4. Slide the marshmallow off the stick and onto the candy bar. (Be careful! The marshmallow will be hot.)
5. Place the other graham cracker on top of the marshmallow (like a sandwich).
6. Eat and say Yummy! I want s'more!

Every animal leaves a unique print or track in the sand, snow, along a dirt trail, or in the moist dirt by the water's edge. Animals don't cover their tracks. They remain as evidence that an animal has traveled through the area.

Look carefully around the camping area to find hoof or paw prints. Think about an animal that lives nearby and find its tracks. Is it a big or small animal? Which direction is it traveling? These clues tell us about animals that live nearby.

Print track books help identify an animal by matching prints with the book's illustrations. If a track book isn't handy, make a sketch of the track and check at the visitor's center to identify which animal made it.

Animals leave other clues that tell they've been in the area including scat (their droppings), antlers, feathers, or hair. Bears leave claw marks on trees. Some animals, including deer, lose their antlers every year to make way for new ones. Become a nature detective and watch for tracks, paw prints, and other animal evidence.

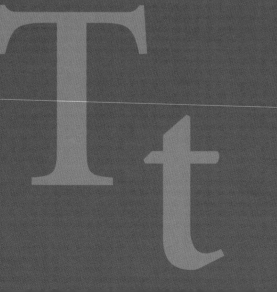

T is for the Tracks we find
         pressed upon the ground.
Traces of our animal friends
         lie waiting to be found.

Campers see a variety of animals on a camping trip—big and small. But there are also animals living underground. Some live completely underground their entire lives. Others have homes below ground, but come out to play or hunt for food. This protects them from weather and predators. Holes are entries to underground homes. Experts can look at a hole and know which animal lives there. Be safe and never bother an animal hole.

Mountain campers might see marmots (MAHR-muts). They are the largest member of the squirrel family and live in underground burrows. Adult marmots are one to two feet long and have long furry tails, short legs, and strong claws for digging. One marmot remains on guard and makes a special call to warn other marmots of intruders. They eat plants and grow fat by fall, and then they hibernate (sleep) through winter in their burrows.

Kangaroo rats live in rocky and sandy desert soil. Their burrows enter the ground at an angle. They stay in their burrows all day and only come out at night when it's cool.

U is for the Underground,
hidden burrows out of sight
dug by those who need a home
safe from harm both day and night.

V is for Views and Vistas
of deserts and forests and sky
with awe inspiring beauty
so pleasing to the eye.

Hikers must stop for breaks to drink water and eat high-energy snacks. This gives their body time to refresh. Breaks are great for admiring the view. Campers watch clouds and notice their changing shapes or find birds soaring in the sky or tucked in a tree. Early risers are treated to a beautiful sunrise and hikers like to watch the sunset.

A pad of paper and pencil in a daypack are handy for sketching. Some campers pack colored pencils or paints. Others write what they do and see each day in their journal. Look carefully and take photographs to remember interesting sights. Sketches, written memories, and photographs can be compiled to make a memory album of a camping adventure. (Directions for making an album are at the back of this book.)

The Blue Ridge Parkway is a popular national parkland. It winds through Virginia and North Carolina connecting Shenandoah and Great Smoky Mountains National Parks. Over 16 million people visit this area each year to camp and stop at overlooks to admire views.

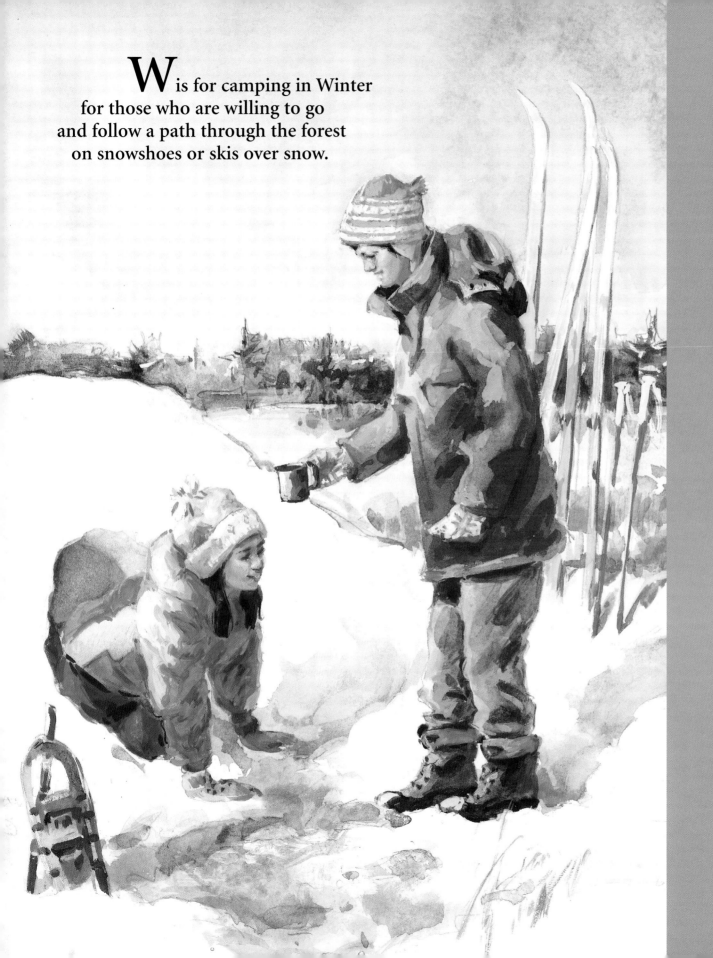

W is for camping in Winter
for those who are willing to go
and follow a path through the forest
on snowshoes or skis over snow.

Winter campers snowshoe, cross-country ski, and ice fish. Shelters might be a tent, an igloo, or a quinzhee (a shelter made by piling snow). Tenters use "dead man stakes" to hold tents secure. To make a "dead man," dig a trench more than a foot deep in the snow at the tent's corner. Place a stick in the trench with a cord from the tent corner under it. Hold the cord's free end and fill the trench with packed snow. Pull to tighten the cord and the tent corner is firmly tied down.

Winter camping requires warm and waterproof clothing. Gaiters cover boots and pants to keep snow out of waterproof boots. A knit hat, gloves, insulating underwear, and jacket are must-haves for every winter gear list.

Campers must prepare for cold nights. Sleeping bags are rated by the lowest temperature in which they'll keep a camper warm. They are identified by which seasons they will be usable. Winter campers need a four-season sleeping bag. Mummy bags are tapered and tight to keep in body heat. They are excellent for winter camping.

W
W

Trail signs help pinpoint a location on a trail map. They mark the direction and distance to a destination. If a trail is not visible, rangers or hikers make "ducks" (stacks of small rocks) to clearly mark the trail. Hikers keep safe by staying on well-marked trails. Hiking off a trail is unsafe, destroys fragile plant life, and causes erosion.

Map reading and pathfinding skills are important to hikers. They navigate by using a map and compass to find their location. To learn to use a map and compass, have the ranger or leader show you where you are on the map. Align the MN (Magnetic North) arrow at the bottom of your map in the same direction as your compass needle. By orienting the map, you can look on the map and see a feature (for example a mountain) and look in the same direction to see it. A topographical (topo) map shows the location of mountains, trails, streams, campgrounds, and other features. It also shows the steepness of the terrain.

Even if you take a GPS (global positioning system) when hiking, you need to take a compass. Using a map and compass helps keep hikers safe.

X
x

X is for two Xing trails.
   Now, which way should we go?
North or south? East or west?
   A trail map helps us know.

Y is for Yellowstone Park
where bison and moose freely roam.
Where Old Faithful spouts every hour,
and bears and elk make their home.

Yy

Located in Wyoming, Montana, and Idaho, Yellowstone was the world's first national park. John Colter was the first white explorer to visit this area. He joined the Lewis and Clark expedition in 1803 and explored the Yellowstone area in 1807.

In 1872 Congress declared it a national park when they saw photographs of its amazing beauty and geothermal wonders. They wanted to preserve this area and protect its fragile resources.

Yellowstone has more hot springs and geysers than any place in the entire world. Old Faithful is Yellowstone's most famous geyser. On average, it erupts about every 74 minutes and shoots steam and boiling water over 100 feet into the air.

Yellowstone is also known for its animals including elk, moose, bison, and bears. An important safety tip for every camping trip is to never approach or feed any wildlife—big or small! Remember: Keep safe and let all animals remain wild.

Zip is the sound campers hear at the end of a camping day. Zippers create doors and windows for tents. A zipper runs down the side and across the foot of a sleeping bag. Warm, clean, and dry sleeping bags filled with down (soft feathers) or other insulating materials keep campers cozy. An insulating pad under a sleeping bag helps keep a camper comfy and even warmer.

When campers are ready to head home, they *break camp* and gather all of their belongings. A campsite should always be left as clean or cleaner than it was when campers arrived.

Follow this motto—"If you packed it in, pack it out." Don't leave anything that shows someone has been camping.

Campers don't need to travel far from home to camp. Backyard camping is fun. It gives you a chance to try out gear and practice putting up a tent. In fact, if you've never camped it's smart to practice camping in your own backyard.

No matter where your camping takes you, you're sure to have excellent camping adventures.

"Take only memories. Leave nothing but footprints." —Chief Seattle

ZZZZZZZZZZZZZZZ

Z is for the Zippers
on your cozy bag and tent.
Nested away, you'll fall asleep
dreaming of places you went.

S'More Camping Fun

Create Your Own Sketch Pad or Memory Book

Before you leave on a camping trip, make a journal to collect camping memories and sketches by following these directions.

Supplies:

- 10-15 pieces of paper (for the inside of the book—they need to be the same size as the cover sheets)
- 2 pieces of heavier paper (for the book's covers)
- 1 rubber band (heavy, size 32 or 33)
- hole punch
- twig (or other long thin item to hold the book together, like a paint brush, pencil, etc.)

1. Put the two heavy sheets of paper on the top and bottom of the other sheets of paper. These will be the book's covers.

2. Punch two holes where you want the spine to be. This will usually be the left side of the book. (Place the holes at least ½" from the edge of your paper and 3" apart.)

3. Start from the back of the book, and thread the end of the rubber band through one of the holes.

4. Put the stick (or other thin item) through the end of the rubber band on the front side of your book.

5. Repeat for the other end of the rubber band in the second hole.

Camp Cuisine

Trail Mix (also called "Gorp")
It's fun and easy to make a healthy trail mix.
Choose a sweet, salty, and crunchy combination.

Here are some suggestions for ingredients:

- raisins
- nuts
- sunflower or pumpkin seeds
- dried fruit (like dried apricots, cranberries, or bananas)
- dry cereal
- pretzels (little ones work best)
- chocolate chips (some people prefer butter-scotch bits)
- shredded coconut

Depending on how much trail mix you want to make, add equal parts of your favorite ingredients to a large mixing bowl. Use a wooden spoon to mix the ingredients together. Divide into snack-size amounts and place in small plastic, sealable bags—just the right size for rest stops on the trail.

Be a No-Impact Camper

- If you take it in, take it out. Don't leave litter. Leave your campsite cleaner than you found it.

- Keep streams and lakes clean. Use biodegradable soap. Don't dump anything in water sources including campsite faucet areas.

- Let wildlife stay wild. Don't feed animals. Properly store your food away from animals.

- Prevent forest fires. Keep your campfire small, never leave it unattended, and keep a debris-free area around the fire. Have water ready to extinguish the fire completely.

- Leave wildflowers, plants, and trees as you found them. Don't pick, cut, or carve them.

- Stay on trails to avoid erosion.

- Follow all of your campsite's rules including "quiet time" rules.